AND YES, THIS TOO

poems by

Laura Pelton-Sweet

Finishing Line Press
Georgetown, Kentucky

AND YES, THIS TOO

ACKNOWLEDGMENTS

Sincere thank you to Ms. Erika Buschmann for use of her artwork "Before
the Storm," ©2004, charcoal and pastel on paper.

Publisher: Leah Huete de Maines
Editor: Christen Kincaid
Cover Art: Erika Buschmann
Author Photo: Michael Sweet
Cover Design: Elizabeth Maines McCleavy

Order online: www.finishinglinepress.com
also available on amazon.com

Author inquiries and mail orders:
Finishing Line Press
PO Box 1626
Georgetown, Kentucky 40324
USA

Contents

This Is How.. 1

Thanks Giving.. 2

How To Become a Poet... 3

Old Man Tomato 4

Lovewell Street Haiku 5

The Measure of Our Sorrows.. 6

Bluebirds... 7

The Weaver.. 8

Altars.. 9

Falling Awake... 10

What It Means (Amor Fati)... 11

Anna... 12

Of The Nature 13

Like This 15

The Catalog 1-8.. 16

Being Human, Together 18

Do Not Disturb, Tiny Grass Is Dreaming*....................... 19

Metta For Weeds... 20

The Wisdom Of Ferns.. 21

Tornado Warning 22

Autumn, Apples.. 23

Beautiful... 24

Thoughts Become Haiku 25

Quietly, Here 26

For Michael:
you are the water to the roots
and the sunlight to the soft green leaves.
You have shown me what it means to be loved.

THIS IS HOW

This is how
it is accomplished:
Just one moment,
and then another.

The two of us
held in place by the piercing
of a delicate pin
through each silky wing,

by pinky-swears,
by the long thread of years,
yours woven into mine,
mine woven into yours,

by these claws gripping
this wire, and
these words circling between us
unspoken.

All we have is this moment
and then this one.
We stay together
by staying together.

THANKS GIVING

Gratitude is a seat at this table.
It is the many gifts
whispered into the still night air,
under pale glow of porchlight
and muted snow, drifting.
"This too, don't forget."
The steam that rises from this offering says
"You've spent your life preparing
this exact feast."

Surely, there is always at least one
uninvited guest, bringing with them
an exhaustion barely contained
by these hands:
A dog-eared tired,
a charred-bones-by-the-edge-of-the-fire tired.
Fear glinting like sun on water,
grief like bruised knees.
These, too, belong at the table.

But there is room for more: a soft smile
that cradles the eyes,
and loving fingers, tangled.
Affection ripe like cherries in spring,
laughter like a lion's roar.
A flaying passion,
a crisp spark in quiet countryside,
and enough hope to propel my heart
forward, forward.

Yes, these too.
This table is strong enough
to hold them all.

HOW TO BECOME A POET

Stop thinking.

Stop thinking, and let yourself feel.
Let the immovable joy
that lies under everything
shake you,
skin and bones.

Hurt,
and hurt again.

Inhabit the house of your life
with hope, fill the rooms
with the best of intentions,
and in the end
fall short of them all.

Attempt to know yourself and realize
that you never fully will.

Realize that you are imperfect,
that you are capable of creating great pain
and great beauty.
You are capable
of much more than you planned.

That skin you are shedding
like a snake's
isn't who you really are.

OLD MAN TOMATO

If a plant can be loyal,
you are.
Your many limbs
like tentacles reaching for every corner
of this space,
once green and optimistic,
now steadily drying, dropping.
Your solid, woody trunk
is mottled with age.
In another's garden
you would have been discarded.
But I treasure your one arm
and one leg,
and your valiant efforts to bloom again,
to offer me these
last
two
tomatoes.

LOVEWELL STREET HAIKU

Passing Lovewell Street,
your hand reaching for my hand.
This moment, just this.

THE MEASURE OF OUR SORROWS

It is as if we have learned nothing,
as if the clear bead at the center
changes nothing and we have to
start at step one again, like infants.
To make mistakes, small and large.
To see again the waves caused by one drop
of our past selves in another,
and to feel anew the full measure
of all the world's sorrows,
residing in this one human heart,
before being able to truly understand.

BLUEBIRDS

Your many sadnesses,
like a flock of bluebirds,
are very welcome
inside the garden of my heart.
I've opened the gate.
Please come inside.

THE WEAVER

Sometimes, life seems so flexible,
an intricate design on a
skillfully woven carpet.
Short, colorful threads standing, bending,
swaying gently to one side
in response to moments of living.
Intention blurring with the slightest pressure,
this breath,
and now this one.

The magic is in the knots.
The real design,
colors nestled into textures,
wool in grease,
strong foundation under disciplined tension.
The real intention visible
only when everything has
finally
been turned upside down.

Sometimes life turns upside down, too,
before we finally learn
how to look.

Look.
The head bows to the heart,
the heart, to the heartbeat,
the warp to the weft.
The pattern of this life is
woven, knotted,
beaten and trimmed into being,
more beautiful and more terrible than
we ever imagined.

ALTARS

~In memory of Neal Brown

Nothing is a small thing
anymore.
That hat, those gloves,
pants hung carelessly
on the back of a door.
Altars now,
each of them,
to a life lived with love
and with more joy than one body
should be able to hold.

FALLING AWAKE

The difference is
three in hours,
almost nine in months,
and just over 2964 in miles.

The wind howls.
Firelight tightens its flickering cloak
around us and the sudden encounter
with a pantheon of gods
who demanded no less
than everything.

WHAT IT MEANS (Amor Fati)

You look at me as if
there is a mystery to be solved,
as if you would like to understand
how the grain of sand becomes a pearl,
how the seed becomes a flower,
but you will settle for
a small, round gleam of light
in the palm of your hand.
Or for the quick, sharp beats of joy,
each staccato moment its own puzzle
shining out from the cracks.

So many cracks. So many grains of sand
whirling like dervishes.
Limbs called to dance.
Your words of love settle into my bones,
and the weight of my own hand
settles over my own heart, a pulsing
of *not alone, not alone, not alone.*
Darkness becoming light becoming
    Joy.

There is a solid thread within me
and between us—it is transformation.
Bison saliva becomes new grass.
New grass becomes new breath.
Breath becomes song becomes fire,
fire becomes sugar becomes skin.
These gifts become gratitude,
signposts of love and darkness,
    equally worthy.

ANNA

Waking from a dream
in which all was forgotten,
in which whatever hurts still exist
between us were set gently aside,
and we were
again
joyful friends.

We played like children,
the aches in our older bodies gone,
the bruises to our older hearts
healed, suddenly, simply.
I know the real world
isn't like that.

The day seems very different
when the sun is up.

OF THE NATURE

Branches break
under the weight of winter ice.
Oak galls, once full of life,
dry and fall.
Soft buds open to the bumblebee,
become fruit, become juice, become mulch.

A voice inside says
"Embrace this mystery.
Your body, too, is of the nature
to fall.
You, too, are of the nature to die."

It is so easy for me to fear this,
to focus on regrets,
on the grasping self,
the part of me
that held the world so tightly it broke.
It's so easy to forget that the lotus
thrives in the sticky mud
of the slow moving current.

"This life is the lotus," the voice says.
"Your mind is of the nature to be curious,
to be patient.
Your soul is of the nature
to grow compassion like seedlings in a greenhouse.
Your heart is of the nature to be loving,
to be grateful,
to become wide enough
for the world to fit inside."

I feel the truth of this
in the warm air, wafting.
In the early morning music that cradles the hillside.
This life is the lotus, messy and impossibly beautiful.
Like this poem, perhaps there is
no clear answer, no tidy package.
Just this moment.

And this one.

And this one.

LIKE THIS

It's like this:
When the charges are read, I still
ache for comfort,
still try to hold myself up, try to
hold onto my blossoms,
like a crape myrtle in a hurricane.
I still try.

And it's also like this:
Good days are sometimes spent waiting
and bad days sometimes spent wishing,
skin and bones cracking under pressure.
Inevitable, it seems.
A deep, rattling breath, underwater.

Then, also, movement,
like this:
A soft smile into the mouth of the storm.
A scrape of carbon
from the toast and we continue the journey.
We are a part of nature.
No part of nature is
constantly in bloom.

THE CATALOG 1-8

One is the smallest smile,
the one that doesn't find your eyes.
Trip-wired and taut,
the only one I saw for awhile.
The tense one that says
"I'm worn out and stretched thin but I swear I'm trying."

Two is lighter in step,
is a sleepy kid,
squints and waves in greeting
on a quiet morning.
Two is playful like a puppy,
wears pajamas, seems unafraid.

Three is unexpected,
fresh air from an open window.
Three cracks your face wide open,
with a barking laugh
and the slow, tousled timbre
of that cowboy who drinks Sarsaparilla.

Four tries hard to be Three.
Wide-eyed, manic,
waylaid on the journey
between thought and deed.

Five seems comfortable,
takes care of me like a friend who
shares his apple,
holds it out fondly, delicately,
for me to take a bite.

Six laughs, sure-footed.
Six laughs at me, delights
at my delight in rusty metal
and farms and Christmas.
Six holds me tight as I laugh at myself.

Seven is proud of us,
and of who we have become.
Sometimes sad, but also amazed
and so damn proud.

Eight is calm and confidence.
Eight says "I love you, Little Bird."
And "I will miss you when you're gone."
And "There are good things to come."

BEING HUMAN, TOGETHER

Don't we all feel
that we live in fraught times?
That ours are the most painful,
or complicated, or difficult?
Has anyone ever lived
asking why this being human
is so easy?

DO NOT DISTURB, TINY GRASS IS DREAMING*

Tiny, tender, fragrant grass,
protected in sleep by a small sign
and a gardener with a kind heart.
Protected by words from crushing steps,
from my own restless heart,
from my yearning to kick off the shoes
and the losses
and wander, barefoot and rebellious,
breathless and defiant.

Is it true, as the man says it is,**
that humanity is a grief club,
that yearning is our universal condition,
and that these are the threads
binding us to each other?
If so, I and the kind-hearted gardener
are bound,
both yearning for an impossible balm
to our restless hearts.
They for the orderly beauty
of tall, undisturbed blades of new green,
and I for the wild wandering,
folding blade after blade under my careless weight.

But what if we are all unquestionably whole?
Me, the gardener, the million blades of grass,
not as delicate as we have feared?
What if none of us can ever actually be crushed
once we discover our true selves
through loving?

*From a whimsical sign sometimes placed on lawns to protect new grass.
**Nick Cave being interviewed by Krista Tippett in 'On Being.'

METTA FOR WEEDS

Under brutal sun,
soil moist from summer's deluge,
I tend the garden
  pull weeds
  create space in the loamy dark for roots of flowers
  and other shades of green.

Then a voice reminds me:
These weeds are beings too.
I stare at the wilting cluster
between my muddy fingers.

There is only one reply.

"May you be at peace.
May you and all beings be at peace."

THE WISDOM OF FERNS

In the deep of summer, pulling vines
off trees with a manic fugue,
I expose the ferns to the light.
Harsh sun withers delicate pinnae,
fronds furling and falling
under the glare of August.
The guilt is a weight
over long winter months,
under the graying sky, but
these rhizomes are wiser and more patient
than I.
They rested while I worried.
Spring comes.
Fiddleheads appear from the moist earth,
and confidently shush me,
saying *"Don't you worry,*
We know what we are doing."

TORNADO WARNING

Inside and outside, sometimes:
unseasonable weather.
The pulse of rain, a heartbeat.
Gaia's lungs expand with mine.
Thunder punches through my ribcage,
lightning pierces my eyelids.

Just breathe.

We shelter
in an old basement bowling alley
while gods and devas
throw rocks upstairs.
The floorboards tremble.

Breathe.
Just breathe.
Birds will sing tomorrow.

AUTUMN, APPLES
~In Memory of Edward Lundy

It's autumn, there should be apples.

There should be apples, red and glossy,
leaves the shape of almonds,
and all the colors of the October hillside.

Instead this tree, like you are,
like we all will,
is deciding there will be no fruit
this winter.

Bluejays and robins,
full-hearted,
wide eyed and colorful,
wait for you on bare, moss covered branches.

The realization happens swiftly.

Sunlight will stretch into every crevice,
across drying bark and skin,
through loving words and wind, rustling.

Sunlight will land here,
making everything it touches
holy, holy.

BEAUTIFUL

In many ways,
by design or default,
by agreement or mere
acceptance we've said
you would go first.

But if by fate or some
cosmic joke it's me,
please scatter my ashes
in all the places you've never seen.

Allow me to do for you
in death what I wanted to do
in life—to show you
all the magnificent corners of the world,
and your place
in each of them.

Let the dew in their cradles
of leaves of every color
sing back to you the truth of things:
    You are strong.
    You are brave.
    You are beautiful.
    You are beautiful.

THOUGHTS BECOME HAIKU

1.
Honored gentlemen,
bees grumble at my presence
like cranky neighbors.

2.
A chorus of frogs,
uncles, chuckling at the past.
They've sure seen some shit.

3.
Many shades of green,
an unknowable number.
We call them all "grass."

4.
Small waves of sadness.
Many causes, no causes.
Just whispers on wind.

5.
Walking amongst trees—
Past, present, no difference.
Grandmothers are here.

6.
Gingko leaves give thanks,
dancing joyfully, mid-air.
The wind answers back.

QUIETLY, HERE

These have no home
at the moment, these carefully formed
and warmly loved phrases,
each leaning like winter branches toward
a moment past,
so I'll place them quietly,
here.

Laura is a seeker. She currently makes her home in Central Massachusetts, with her husband of 26 years and many non-human beings. She aims to leave each day better than she found it, through quiet reflection, tending plants, making art from discarded objects, and offerings of loving-kindness. Laura is also a licensed mental health counselor and has worked to support the growth of other seekers since 2006.

Her poetry is part of a pattern that reflects life as a therapist, someone who has been given the gift of others' stories. Her work also generally draws from life as an imperfect person, a curious person, a spiritual person, a creative person, a bisexual person in a committed opposite-sex relationship, and a person who hurts. Through poetry, she tries to share all too human experiences of love, fear, loss, grief, and hope. When not writing, Laura may be found doing yoga, watering plants, cooking without recipes, and making jewelry from found bits of rusty metal.

www.ingramcontent.com/pod-product-compliance
Lightning Source LLC
Chambersburg PA
CBHW022058080426
42734CB00009B/1404